T0096433

Boy Running

for Charlie

Boy Running

Paul Henry

SEREN

Seren is the book imprint of
Poetry Wales Press Ltd.
57 Nolton Street, Bridgend, Wales, CF31 3AE

www.serenbooks.com
facebook.com/SerenBooks
twitter@SerenBooks

The right of Paul Henry to be identified as
the author of this work has been asserted in accordance
with the Copyright, Designs and Patents Act, 1988.

ISBN: 978-1-78172-226-8
e-book: 978-1-78172-227-5
Kindle: 978-1-78172-229-9

A CIP record for this title is available from the British Library.

The publisher acknowledges the financial assistance of the Welsh Books Council.

Book Cover: painting by James Donovan.

Author website: www.paulhenrypoet.co.uk

Contents

I. Studio Flat

II. Kicking the Stone

III. Davy Blackrock

What is my house but a flight of wings?
— Julian Orde 'The Changing Wind'

I
Studio Flat

Usk

So we've moved out of the years.
I am finally back upstream
and, but for their holiday grins
on every bookcase, the boys
were never born, it was a dream.
Here is where my past begins

in a garret beside a bridge,
woken by birds pecking moss
from the dark. The river's clear.
It will not turn to sludge
till it reaches you and the mess
of streets I hated, endured

only because you were there.
My windows are full of leaves.
There are mountains in my skylight.
Perhaps you would like it here.
It is the same river – it moves,
perhaps, towards the same light.

Moving In

I cannot see the flowers at my feet...
　　　　　　Keats – 'Ode to a Nightingale.'

They look and wonder what they're doing here,
those who've moved with me across the years –
Dylan Thomas, Picasso, Nightingale Ann,
Goble, David Trevorrow, young Fanny Brawne...
all strewn about this flat where I hide.
(Did I dream, last night, of a tide
laying its artefacts on sand?) They stare
but do not judge, or change, or care.

Dylan's just opened Manhattan's cigar box.
'Try one,' he says, 'before you die. Fuck books.'
Pablo's still pushing against his pane.
He listens for a nightingale in vain.
Goble tilts back in his top hat.
He and Trevorrow could not have shared a flat
but I loved them both, and Fanny Brawne.
There are crows on my roof. The light has gone.

Studio Flat

Socks hang like bats from a skylight.
They may be dry in time for the moon.
The camp site owner's water-feature
drains more blood from the sun.

Cars queue for the narrow bridge.
Birds catch their pulses and fly.
I am suddenly old. What's an attic
but a bungalow in the sky.

And where are you, my sons?
I heard your voices in the bells
of snowdrops pulled by the wind.
These tulips have lost their smell.

Perhaps I could tell you, one day
where the snowdrops went, why old men
dry their socks on the moon, and what
darkened the skylight, just then.

Ring

I can't get the ring out of my finger.
How long till it disappears
this ghost ring, twenty years deep?
I'm branded. Is it the same with you?
Your fingers were slenderer than mine.

Piano

First shame, then guilt, then a piano –
you left me this piano.
It strikes me I buried you inside it.

I lift its lid
and all my childhood songs fly out.

The Bright Room

Every night you turned away,
your back a door closing on me,
untouchable, over and over
on the hinges of four seasons,
your dark door closing on the years.

And what did it matter
in *Orontes*, our first house,
where not one door closed properly?
The sash windows lifted enough
then seized

        and if we argued
one of us would slam a door
and lean against it, while the other
pushed until, more often than not
the stalemate, the stubborn curses
on either side of the door
would turn to laughter and the door
would join in as it gave
and light poured back in.

The snowdrops came and went
in the garden. The boys grew
too tall for their beds....

           Last night
I rose up the steps of *Orontes*,
rang the bell. The green door stuck
before it opened. *I've lost my keys.*
You smiled, then frowned
then stared through me,
through the seasons, the years,
into this bright, empty room.

Chattels

The trolley with a twang in its drawer.

The chattels of love, the chattels of war.

The tawny dining table's wings
clipped, as if cutlery never sang

to the dresser with the spinning chip
that kept mysterious its door.

The chattels of love, the chattels of war.

The metronome's pyramid
on the dusty piano lid.

                    The keys
without furniture, on the floor.

The chattels of love, the chattels of war.

The standard lamp's missing claw.

The gramophone that winds up
Paul Robeson singing *Water Boy*
(*the Convict Song*) once more.

The chattels of love, the chattels of war.

From a matchbox, this lock of hair
the sunlight suddenly saw.

And, at the end of five rainbows
five medals nobody wore.

The chattels of love, the chattels of war.

Hour

Here is the hour that gave up on sleep.
I should like to give it to you
for Christmas, its gentle thaw
beneath a scrawny lamp, its slope
the snow slides off, at last
in blocks, sledging down the slate.
Here is the ticking away of its weight.
May it lighten your sleeping coast.

Is this the closest I can get
to holding you? Listen... more ice
falls into the sea. By the day
this hour reaches you, the planet
will have forgotten it. Turn your face
to me now, let the sheets fall away.

Seven Twenty-Five

As good a time as any
to fall out of love.

I haven't wound this clock
for days – your silence
silenced its chimes.

Dead clock. Dead
as the old man's heart
in that song.

Either I wind it now
and believe there is time
beyond seven twenty-five

believe that cogs and springs
will dance again

or I post you this key.

Jo

A woman irons the river Usk
under my bedroom. Brought to her
in plastic bags, by the elderly
she smooths out the creases, patiently,
smooths out the years, folds them,
hands them back a simpler river.

Her steamed-up surgery never rests.
Sometimes when I wake I hear
an otter's mating call, ducks,
dippers, a fisherman's 'Yes!',
a drowning child crying for help....
All of the river's griefs and joys are hers.

And sometimes, when my weather-vane's fox
creaks at night, the dead, in dripping shirts
and heavy frocks, rise up
from the river's tabernacle and knock-
knock on Jo's glass door.

Jones, Powell, Prosser, Price...
her *Closed* sign means nothing to them.
They want to see themselves again
in Sunday best, in the river's glass.
'Jo! Jo!', they cry. 'Are you there? Jo?'

The Picture Framer

They bring their babies to him,
their watercolour hills and vases,
their offspring in caps and gowns....

Surfacing from his windowless shop
he blinks and blinks at the sun,
crouches against his wall
like a miner

                        draws on a roll-up's
smoke signal, invisible
to the queuing cars at the bridge,
their village portraits in profile

which he studies, vanishing
in the puff of a truck's exhaust.

Slipping in and out of his frame
he is free to be ghostly,
to open and close as he chooses.

Only a field's gilded hedge
holds him now, as he drifts across
a landscape too vast to contain.

To The Landlord

for Oliver Reynolds

I should like to complain
about the man in the upstairs flat.
He is too quiet.
His thoughts are deafening.
When he grinds his teeth
my windows rattle.
The sky darkens when he closes his eyes.
He scratches his head
and a low-flying jet
scrapes across the village.
He scratches his balls
and the bulls go wild in their fields.
How can I massage my clients
with his silence raging above?
I am starting to lose sleep,
to exist at the pit of a well
his pious smile peers into.
My regulars are deserting me.
Only yesterday, a prayer's wing
(it must have been his)
repeated itself on the pane.
He turns a page and a gust of wind
blows my sign into the road.
He wants to destroy me.
Get him to a monastery.
His doorbell's broken. I knock
his floor with a long broom
but he never knocks back.
What happened to that family
with the head-lice? I miss their screams.

The Landlord's Painting

I misread the painting all along.
The phallus is a thigh,
the second phallus an umbilical cord.
It is the agony of birth,
a monstrous Madonna and child,
a tuberous father at their side –
three plants howling at the sky
in a garden gone wild.

What will grow when the cord is cut?
Let it be good. Let it
find the sun between leaves.
Let eager shoots escape the earth
and blossom into song and, trembling
find a new colour for love.

No Pets Allowed

So I walk Milo Morgan,
the boxer from the garage
who is stronger than Milo of Croton,
whose muscle no gym articulates,
who could shit for Wales,
who snorts and salivates
a snail trail down my jeans.
More of a spaniel man
I walk Milo Morgan
who turns into a motorboat
I ski behind, on grass
when he spies a stray sheep.

I tie him to a bench by the Usk.
We are getting used to each other.
He barks at the low-flying ducks.
I walk Milo Morgan.
There is beauty in a crushed expression.
The same sun warms his face and mine.

Note. 'Milo of Croton': legendary Grecian athlete and soldier who won six Olympic wrestling championships, starting from the 60th Olympics in 540 BC.

Under the River

Under the river a deeper river runs.
It is simply a case of pressing your ear
your heart to the bank, about here,
then of listening to its quieter turns

to the voices of loved ones
you thought would never rise again,
holding you now, with an old refrain.
Under the river a deeper river runs.

★

Into the dimming light the fish stone,
the flit-spirits, the singing well,
the sudden bleat festival.
And the white manor's sloping lawn

is a tennis court on the run. Rain
salts its lines, makes bull's eyes
of trout kisses. *O... o... O...*
Into the dimming light the fish stone.

★

Some of us are ghosts before we die,
dressing too darkly in summer,
following church bells in winter
down crumbling staircases of sky

to the river, where a deeper river lies
about here. Hush, they are singing well
tonight, as we are singing still
though some of us are ghosts before we die.

The Dog in the Reeds

The vagaries of light sustained me
when I lived in the city for you –
the brush-and-go of a sheet
on a window, the summer's last card
dealt onto a paving stone, a railing's
sudden alchemy.... It was enough.
A warm brick in a terrace was love,
a back yard's chandelier of pears.

And when the light wouldn't play
I'd walk old Alfie down the river.
He'd shake on his frame in the mud,
milky eyed and pissing blood
and deaf, lost in the tall reeds,
hair blown about his sunken hull.
He'd shiver and sniff at the setting sun
when I called his name... *Alfie!*

Small boats pulled at their leads,
their rosaries of barrels and tyres.
Esther, on the bank, on blocks
would have done for you and me
and the boys, and Alfie –
big enough to live and breed in,
to leak laughter and light. *Alfie!*

To what oceans did we aspire
beyond the love of a rescued dog?

The night I sailed, he howled
about the house, unable to find us,
to tell us where he'd buried the years.

If you peer through this porthole,
this one   you may still see me
or hear me, cursing in the dark,
lost, knee-deep in moonlight

whistling for our dog in the reeds.

Have You Seen Sonny?

The way cats sometimes take off,
old cats even, into a darkness
beyond their owner's cries,
to join the wind's strays
ghosting in and out of the flap,
leaving it all behind – the crap
in the litter tray, the hair
that sticks to the furniture,
the LOST poster's faint whiff
of a slave master's disbelief...

and the way it still beckons us
with moonlight, that gap
in the garden hedge, as if
it were not too late
to slip through its wires,
find ourselves on the other side.

House

Did we carry it in our dreams?
Or were we the figurines
the sun's eye peered into?

We shall never own it again
and would not want to,
though we still dream of its rooms.

Boy Running

for Ioan

The canal tilts him back and fore
like a boat in a toy pen
or the bubble in a spirit-level
that never quite finds its middle.

There are worse ways to grow tall
under the rustling sun and rain
between bridges 14 and 21

to outlive an owl, a drake, a hawk
where no two leaves blow the same way
and pumpkin lanterns moor for the night.

Run, boy running, run
past the sighing old man
and his blind Labrador,
the foal in her wire necklace.

Run, between east and west,
spring and autumn, dawn and dusk.
Is it your breath now or mine
deep inside your chest?

There are worse ways to never settle
in full flight, to be loved.
Run, my shadow, run.
Run but always stay in sight.

An owl cries, deep inside the trees.
The canal's glass is full of moonlight.

St Julia's Prayer

I've closed the skylight for the night.
I hope that your prayer slipped in
in time and was not too exhausted
from its flight, and that it is here
hovering about these pieces of me
which I would sing to you now
if they sounded like home.

The lamplight makes me monstrous
on the far wall. Perhaps your prayer
forgives such ugliness, my soul
become frightening at this hour.
Can you hear the sea from your room?
I imagine I will hear it too
if I press my ear to your prayer
when I find it.

Where is it?
All these shadows smother it
and the shadow of this hand on the wall.
But I sense it here, your prayer
and I shan't open the skylight till dawn.

A flock of bells...

A flock of bells takes the air
and you come to me, out of nowhere

and I smile, knowing you'll visit me
always, that this is how it will be

till the last thread of an island
slips through a bell-ringer's hands

and they put me in the listening earth.

The See-saw

All night, two women of equal weight
on a see-saw, one fair-haired, one dark,
the balance not resting once.

                         All night
the two, staring into each other's eyes
as ghosts might

                   the breeze they create
lifting, in turn, a fringe, a hem...

Legs bend, straighten...   Neither lets go
of the steel rein.

                  Long after he's buried,
the dreamer, deep as the fulcrum
between them

                between their clockwork
rising and falling, he'll love them
equally.

The Early City

The night has not yet broken
their sighs, nor have they moved
to stranger rooms, my sleeping sons.

They are not yet differently loved
but dream now, inside this rain,
inside the old time again.

Late Kick-off

My boys are coming back to me
across the Glebelands pitches
out of the echoey underpass
leaving their childhoods behind
on the other side of the motorway

letting our ghosts play on
into the dark, the four of us
hoofing the moon high,
our heads tilted, and staggering
like drunks to catch it,
waiting for it to fall...
the brightest ball in the sky
lighting our way home.

They are coming back to me
taller than I imagined
and too old to warm inside my fleece.
It has been too long.
They must be cold by now.
I'll warm up the engine.

I remember when the plastic goals
they used to pack, at full-time
into sacks (and bear shoulder high
like fathers, or dead kings,
back to the club-house)
were exchanged for serious steel.
After that they needed me less
and less

          but look!
They are coming back to me.
Though it was I who went away.

II

Kicking the Stone

Kicking the Stone

for Peter and Helen

ahead of the shadow I cast,
up the unfinished road
from The Batchelor's to 58.
O scuff of sunny dust.

A dog barks in time.
Psychedelic flowers sprawl
across Mary Coffee's wall.
A woman sings my name.

★

In place of graves, front doors
name the neighbours –
Colin & Heather, Wyn & Mair
Wendy & Rose, The Bachelor...

and underneath, the year
1969. The stone
can't slip into the drain
outside Mary Coffee's

or all of the hinges
on all of the doors
open their lids
with a deafening roar.

★

The Bachelor's in the boot
of his latest *Anglia*,
testing the suspension.
He keeps on his cap and coat.

Its bumper drives the sun
through Heather's kitchen blinds
and into her fruit bowl,
then out and up again

and through a nasturtia leaf
in Wyn Kyffin's rockery.
The stone, at this second
is less sphere, more diamond

but it flies, more or less,
where my right foot
and sometimes my left tells it,
up the unfinished road.

★

One down from The Bachelor's
the bungalow without a name.
The stone pauses in the gap
at the brow of its sloping drive.

A bicycle sleeps on its side,
its back wheel still spinning,
its rider somewhere else.
Tick, tick, tick, tick...

Someone has mowed the lawn
when nobody was looking.
The sun's wheel squeaks
with gulls. Do I dare to

ring a bell? The window's nets
are dancers holding their breath
for decades, or at least until
the stone has danced on.

★

The stone lands perfectly
outside Wendy & Rose's
but rolls back on the rise
towards me. I kick it again

before it has time to settle.
It lands in the same place
almost, then trickles down
once more towards me.

This time I kick it hard
and it clears the drain lid
that brings out the ants
when you stamp on it.

The gutter shades the stone
which has skewed off course
and waits to be rescued.
Why did I choose it? –

this stupid, wayward stone
that might vanish at any

★

The chalky moon in the blue
waits for the stone,
waits for Menna Kyffin's kite
to jump over it

                    red

over the beehives and slacks,
the paisley ties and corduroys,
the shared borders of lawns...
Menna Kyffin's kite

                    red

against the chalky moon
in the blue, as the stone
takes its time and thinks
it is no more grey than

                    red

up the steepish bit between
Mary Coffee's flaking wall
and the Clay's – grey stone
on its arc to the moon.

                    ★

There's hardly time for the stone
to look up and turn
the go-kart racing towards us
into Mary Coffee's trolley.

Its brakes don't work.
Its scones wear goggles,
hold the tatted doilies down.
Its casters laugh, hysterically

as they round the barking bend.
They will not stop –
Heather, Wendy, Mary, Mair...
until they reach the sea.

Heather's in her kitchen.
The Bachelor's in his boot.
I stroke a caterpillar's fur
on Mary Coffee's wall.

A cardboard dalek waves
on its way to Rhoshendre.
Wyn Kyffin skips in his drive.
The heavenly stone arcs on

in small and giant leaps
ahead of the shadow I cast.
Over a lunar landing it picks
a goal for Waunfawr Wanderers.

*

Stone, I think I saw you fall
from Constitution Hill.
Wandering under the cliff
after fishing for ghost fish

I must have taken pity on you,
brought you home, kicked you
all the way up Penglais Hill
then into Maeshendre

where I kick you this minute
between a skipping rope's
first orbit of Wyn Kyffin
and its last, stone without end.

★

Or, biding your centuries
stone, you were always here,
mole-like under the reeds,
when houses were an idea.

The bubbling of a lark
over the heathered marsh
may have disturbed your sleep,
brought light to the dark.

★

Wendy swings her bad leg
and wears an old man's suit.
The dragon on her tie
yn casau Saesneg.

*Why is Wendy's hair
parted like Prince Carlo's?*
The stone dribbles past her
in search of an answer.

★

Rose kick-starts her scooter.
Her giant's knee is grazed
from the last great fall.
Her goggles are serious.

They cannot see the stone
who is four million today
and nutmegs Wendy who waves
Rose away down the hill.

I do not yet know or care
that there is nothing clever
about kicking a time piece.
I simply know it is here.

★

Hello Menna, hello Siân
spinning like cogs on a wire,
a red and yellow blur
between concrete posts

between the musical house
and the Clay's. At night
we are all quietly still
as fireworks in boxes.

★

Coming down from the Clay's
Whistling Alan passes through me
and the stone I kick
passes through Whistling Alan.

His whistle is nearer birdsong
than a boy's but neither.
His thin cheeks go out and in
until the music stops.

Whistling Alan never looks up
and the stone is too quick
through his bird cage
as he passes through me.

★

The wasp I spat at in the bin
outside the Waun shop
catches up with the stone
and stings me on the lip.

★

Wendy & Rose are having a row.
Wendy & Rose are having it now.

All of the hinges
on all of the doors
open their lids
with a deafening roar.

★

Priestly in duffel coats
the quiet Clay children
next door to the Kyffin's
are reading *Look and Learn*.

They must be hot by now
unless it is the winter inside
when they slide down the road
wide-eyed on white pillows.

The stone passes their house
and knows they can't hide
forever, hears each page
turning, each breaking wave.

★

Stone, I almost forgot
that I was kicking you!
Like Elis Workman forgets
the trowel is not his hand.

He stirs his cauldron of tar,
lets me share his flask.
Soon the road will be finished
and the other stones buried

but not the chosen stone
whose moment is this road.
Elis will stay in the shade
of his creaking builder's hut

with a darkness in his smile.
The steam roller in the nettles
will not start but shrink
to a rusty toy.

       And stone,
so long as I kick you
this uneven dusty rise
is the sun's rubble to build on.

*

Colin's clean *Beetle* shines.
Before he dies I forget
to tell him that the stone,
no matter how many times

I kick it, stays on this rise
between Mary Coffee's
and the Clay's – dear Colin,
the last name to die

to set up home again
with Heather, inside the cloud
of a *Ladybird* book. Can you hear
the *Beetle's* engine now

powering the white cumulus?
It's where the luggage should be
as Colin takes out a suitcase
from the front, and Heather

unwraps the crockery, a bowl
which is too bright to look at.

*

The stone leaves its scars –
on the end of my shoe,
on Rose's torn knee,
on Wyn & Mair's block floors...

It is the crack in Heather's bowl,
the scratch on the coffee trolley,
on the *Beetle* and the *Anglia*,
the graze a kite leaves in the blue.

It is the one white hair
in Siân's ginger dizziness,
a duffel coat's missing toggle,
Whistling Alan's sore throat,

the curse inside Wendy's leg
that Rose cannot translate.
It is *EW '69*
in a pool of spilt cement.

★

Inside the musical house
a soprano rehearses –
I wonder as I wander
out under the sky…

O scuff of sunny dust,
preserve this woman's song
only the stone and I can hear
up the unfinished road.

Preserve this woman's song
that finds the sea in a stone
as we pass by, up the road,
up the unfinished song.

Wardrobe Time

Come close, Catrin Sands.
Inside wardrobe time
we can still hear them singing –
Edith Smart, Nightingale Ann,
Geta, Heulwen, St Julia....

And Gwyneth Blue is crying
to hear a wardrobe sing in its tomb
with such... gusto!

                    Come close
Catrin Sands. A hanger's metronome
tocks after the door has closed.
Hold onto me, while you can
and keep us dry from the rain
before life finds us again.

I'll keep my black umbrella,
you keep your black *Mercedes*
but it would have been a fair
swap, inside wardrobe time.

And don't... look at me like that
with Gwyneth Blue's eyes
under the drenched petals of your hat.

Come close, Catrin Sands.
We can still hear them singing
in Maeshendre, inside wardrobe time.
It is still pouring *Ave Maria*
through a key-hole's arch of light.

Brown Helen on Harbour Beach

Look down, Brown Helen
from Glanmor Terrace,
from Tabernacle.

The bay's shadow
has found you
but not your teenage ghost.

She waves up at you
from the shoreline

which breaks its promises
at her feet, but look...

in a yellow beach dress
she is waving back to you.

A stray gull on the wind
steers its handlebars inland

and then, unsteadily

back out to sea.

I have anchored my love
this far out (can you see?)

where only the dolphins
and mermaids hear

when I call your name.

Look down from the railing.
The years have
slipped their mooring

but the sun keeps you in its pool.

You scoop up its fire
and pour it back, into the hour
you stand in to keep cool.

Summer on summer
you scoop up its fire.

★

Aur y byd na'i berlau ma-an....

Voices on the tide's wing.
Who are they singing for
Helen, in Tabernacle?

I name these sea voices:

Gwyneth Blue, Catrin Sands,
Geta, Nightingale Ann....

Forty years or more
on the tide's wing.
Who are they singing for?

Look down, Brown Helen.
Is that you, leaving the quay?

Yours was a dazzling hour –
the flash of a mermaid's tail.

The bay fills the chapel porch
so the barque passing
through its arch

might be setting sail.

III
Davy Blackrock

Davy Blackrock

after Ceiriog

'Cariwch, 'medd Dafydd, fy nhelyn i mi,
Ceisiaf cyn marw roi tôn arni hi...'

Beyond the crowded bed
satellite dishes, begging bowls
in the rain, tilt heavenwards

the wind's wolf howls
for Davy Blackrock –
star of an ashen town.

The tower block sways.
Don't look down.

High on his pillow,
his antique clocks,
his Byron, Keats and Shelley

he imagines a past
with both feet on the ground.

His fingers bleed on the frets.
He hits the top A flat.

The pleasure boat in his eyes
has drifted out to sea.

Enough... enough... enough...
whisper the tired waves.

Sleep, Blackrock, on a sea bed
with a shoal of clocks.
Dream your perfect song.

We have heard the workings
of your heart, heard
the singer become the song.

And when you surface,
into the spotlight

let drowned Shelley rise
with Keats's poems in his chest

let the sky clear again,
let the first song you sing
be 'Dafydd y Garreg Wen'.

Blackrock Asleep

A tap warbles all night
in Blackrock's flat
where the mice have wings.

A duet of running water
and birdsong comforts him
as water comforts stone.

He is neither old nor young.
He will ghost through the night
as water over stone.

Blackrock: the Bedsit Years

The lost years owned a rent book
and sometimes fell behind.
Damp, second-hand,
they clung to what they took,
sang between cracked walls,
had plans, murdered mice,
came and went, imprecise
in their choice of doorbells.

The snow made the town its squat,
unshiftable by first light
but the years knew to wait.
In garrets summer forgot
they worked at loneliness
until it fitted, somewhere
behind the eyes – that stare
of no fixed address.

Beyond the locked doors
of murky landings, they shivered
to *The Carnival is Over,*
Another You… by The Seekers,
eventually found themselves
in someone else's face,
a two-up, two-down palace
with a double bed, and bookshelves.

They slipped a silver ring
onto Blackrock's finger. It shone
when he played to his children,
up and down the neck as he sang
with a black guitar on his knee.
But they hid in his dreams,
the years, biding their time,
the dust on the attic's LPs.

The first child flew, the second.
Come back, carnival years!
If I should lose your love dear...
sings the fire to the wind.
And the lost years are calling,
the mousehole bedsits, the sex.
Inside a stairwell's vortex
Blackrock is falling, falling....

Bride of Blackrock

She turned over,
back to the tide.

The sand's vertebrae
went on for miles.

★

She showed him her scars.
He kissed them.

His lips started to bleed.

★

She opened the skylight
and the stars

slid into his eyes.

★

She uncoiled the snake
from her dangerous hair.

It took her a year.

★

She rolled her own prayers

left them on the air.

★

She laced his reins
with forget-me-nots

before each tour.

Blackrock on Tour

Where has he woken now?

                    'It is some kind of
fictional place... As in dreams things are out front that
are concealed in other hotels....'

                        The billowing of words
and the billowing of snow on the street below.

Was it this room, was it, where he almost died?
The mirror keeps its secret. The mousetrap by the cooker
holds back its answer. Who nursed this whisky glass?

The desk clerk's a Hopper. His bouffant was brighter in fifty-three.
Blackrock takes off his shades. The hotel's wearing its own.

The lobby's installations tap their groins all day,
affect indifference.

               The veneration in the red beret
asks him to dance. He drinks and drinks to her spirit.

There are two double beds – one for his conscience,
one for his ego.

            Hear that song he's writing
with his mother's ashes under his nails and his lover's blood
on the sheet?

           The billowing of words and the billowing
of snow on the street.

            The plumbing is wild as ever.
It thunders into dreams, an airlock's sledge hammer
knock-knock-knocking girders into his back.

Did you hear that scream? He has fallen down its stairwell
again, seen the empty frames exhibited on its walls.

All night the window snows, a Stars and Stripes billows
across West 23rd, a dangled sheet reads
Bring Back the Bards.

The billowing of words
and the billowing of snow on the street below.

Note. st. 2. Arthur Miller: 'The Chelsea Affect'.

Segovia Moon

The moon's a guitar.
It hangs in a tilted sky,
strumming the tides in and out.

Couples stare up and listen
for the promised chord.

Night after night they return
for what their parents heard
or said they heard.

To think, a man's fingers
danced on that grain!

A boy looks for a face,
taps his feet, without knowing
without knowing

under the guitar's moon.

A cow jumps over a guitar.
A violin meows.

A wide-eyed doll
cups her ear
in a blue bay window.

Listen...

    a bright guitar

pauses on the wires of song.

Song of a Wire Fence

Once I loved a woman
with barbed wire dreams
and scars ploughed into her skin.
She almost slept in my arms,
she almost slept in my arms.

> And I sang her *Dafydd y Garreg*
> and *Bugeilio'r Gwenith Gwyn*
> from the harps of Capel Curig
> to the hooves of Synod Inn.

I gave her a young man's stare
the night she read my palm,
my fingers ploughed her wild hair
and she almost slept in my arms,
she almost slept in my arms.

> And I sang her *Tros y Garreg*
> and *Ar Hyd y Nos*
> from the floods of Pencarreg
> to the sands of Ynyslas.

The song of a wire fence
crossed over a thousand farms
and love, she knew no distance,
she almost slept in my arms,
she almost slept in my arms.

The Love Songs of Davy Blackrock

The songs I had are withered
Or vanished clean,
Yet there are bright tracks
Where I have been...
        Ivor Gurney – 'The Songs I Had'

Few remembered them
but by the end
it was enough
that they'd brought love,
some good friends.
What was ambition
after all but the drum
of rain on a glass room,
a distraction from the moon?

He'd sit late for hours, Davy
in those final days,
inventing new chords
in his conservatory,
oblivious to the news,
worrying less about words
than the melody,
trusting his ear,
not counting the bars

and, between downpours,
keeping one eye on the stars.

Curse & Bark

Blackrock is on the streets.
What went wrong?
He shuffles in white rags,
screams at a pigeon
between *GAP* and *NEXT*.

Two cranes form an arch
against the horizon.
Their cradles are still,
empty. What they built
rose to meet them.

Blackrock begs in a porch.
Let's give him a dog
to warm his legs –
Nipper, the terrier
from *His Master's Voice*.

They can busk, a double act,
Curse & Bark.

All across the city
there are voices without songs.

Strange Hand

Blackrock the boy is skimming stones
with his old man. Each stone hops
a step further than the one before.
The sun's cold needle has sewn
their echoes into the pines.
Not yet wishing his father dead
Blackrock nuzzles into the wool
that softens a frightening shadow.
And when the good stones run dry
he scales the bank for more and deals
his palm onto a thorn, and cries.

Davy, what are you crying for?

Blackrock the man sits up
in his bed: *Father, old man,
I am crying for the pool of blood
in this strange hand, the lifeline
which you scarred, the bloodline
which is part yours and part mine.*

Lord of the Skylights

Blackrock inspects his clouds,
his infinite acres

Virga
Cirrus, Cirrocumulus
Cirrostratus, Cumulus...

won by years of hard dreaming.

Stratus, Stratocumulus...

Just listen to those pastures sing!

Blackrock's Number One

Between a hammer and a drill
Blackrock is writing another song.
For the twenty minutes it takes
he is young, the only one
to have written the song
with fillers like "just" and "so"
and "yeah" and

                        so it goes on –
between a thousand hammers
and a thousand drills –
a thousand Blackrocks
writing the same song.

His smoky nets are darkening.
He peers out onto Neville Street.
The woman who says *Ta ra,*
Ta ra, Ta ra sweeps her yard.
In a bare, municipal tree,
a pigeon impersonates
a carving of itself.

                        On the sill
another postcard –

                        Dear Davy,
that tune you dreamt, it sounds
familiar.

            I keep this flame
which you can't see, in a window
at 'Garreg Du'.

            Don't be long.

Song

after Kaleem Ajiz

Out of the heart's instrument, this song
remembered by heart, this song.

However badly we played our love,
slipped out of key, this song.

It will not forget us, haunts us now,
plays us into the dusk, this song.

Notes

The 'Davy Blackrock' poems:

Dafydd y Garreg Wen (David of the White Rock), alias Dafydd Owen (1711-1740), was the blind, (as legend has it) eighteenth-century harpist and composer who lived at 'Y Garreg Wen' farm, near Morfa Bychan in Gwynedd.

Known locally as Dafydd y Garreg Wen, Owen called for his harp on his deathbed and played the haunting melody he claimed to have dreamt on a hill between Borth y Gest and Pentrefelin. In the absence of a harpist at his funeral, the congregation hummed Owen's tune, partly fulfilling his last wish that it be performed at his funeral in Ynyscyhaearn. His gravestone dates him as older than his twenty-nine years.

Nearly a century later, the poet Ceiriog (John Ceiriog Hughes; 1832-1887) wrote the Welsh words for the song which, under the title 'Dafydd y Garreg Wen', dramatised Owen's last act. Dafydd y Garreg Wen had become his song.

There are many vocal and instrumental recordings of 'Dafydd y Garreg Wen'. Arrangements include those by Haydn and Britten.

Acknowledgements

Agenda, The Best British Poetry 2012 (Salt, ed. Roddy Lumsden), *The Guardian, New Welsh Review, The North, Planet, Poetry Review, Poetry Wales, The Spectator, Ten Poems from Wales — Fourteen Centuries of Verse & The Twelve Poems of Christmas* (Candlestick Press, ed. Carol Ann Duffy), *The Times Literary Supplement*.

The poem 'Studio Flat' was broadcast on BBC Radio 4's *Poetry Please* though first appeared in *The TLS*. 'Usk' answers 'Sold', the last poem in *Ingrid's Husband*, my previous collection.

I am grateful to my editor, Amy Wack, and to my friend, Stephen Knight, for their help with shaping this collection. Its completion was also assisted by a 'Published Writer's Bursary' from Literature Wales.

Also by Paul Henry

Time Pieces
Captive Audience
The Milk Thief
The Slipped Leash
The Breath of Sleeping Boys & other poems
Ingrid's Husband
Mari d'Ingrid (tr.Gérard Augustin)
The Brittle Sea: New & Selected Poems
The Black Guitar: Selected Poems (India)